UNITED STATES
SUPREME COURT
LIBRARY

Supreme Court Book

by Paul J. Deegan

Published by Abdo & Daughters, 6535 Cecilia Circle, Edina, Minnesota 55439.

Copyright © 1992 by Abdo Consulting Group, Inc., Pentagon Tower, P.O. Box 36036, Minneapolis, Minnesota 55435. International copyrights reserved in all counties. No part of this book may be reproduced in any form without written permission from the publisher. Printed in the United States.

Photo credits: Archive Photos-cover, 5, 6, 9, 15, 28, 31,
                   FPG International-38
                   UPI/Bettmann-11, 17, 19, 32, 40, 42, 44

Edited by: Bob Italia

Library of Congress Cataloging-in-Publication Data

Deegan, Paul J., 1937-
     Supreme Court book / written by Paul Deegan ; [edited by Bob Italia].
        p. cm. — (Supreme Court justices)
     Includes index.
     Summary: A brief explanation of the origin of the Supreme Court, its composition, and how it works.
     ISBN 1-56239-097-X (lib. bdg.)
     1. United States. Supreme Court—Juvenile literature. [1. United States. Supreme Court.] I. Italia, Robert, 1955- . II. Series.
     KF8742.Z9D44   1992
     347.73'26—dc20
     [347.30735]
                                                                    92-13715
                                                                       CIP
                                                                        AC

Table of Contents

Page

4   Little Known but Most Powerful

10   Role of the Court

14   Becoming a Justice

20   The Senate's Role

22   Lifetime Terms

24   American Courts

26   U.S. Legal System

27   Chance of High Court Review Slim

36   Is a Court's Decision Forever?

39   Famous Justices

46   The Court Today

49   Glossary

50   Index

Little Known but Most Powerful

These nine persons are the most powerful people in the United States legal system. Yet their daily routines are unfamiliar even to other government workers in Washington D.C. Most of their work is done in secret.

Two-thirds of Americans surveyed could not name a single one.

When 1992 began, eight of these people were men, one of whom was black. One was a woman. They are the Chief Justice and the Associate Justices of the United States Supreme Court. They have the authority to overrule a decision of the President. They can overturn a law passed by Congress or a state legislature.

The Constitution of the United States was signed on September 17, 1787.

The Supreme Court was established by The Constitution of the United States. This famous document was signed on September 17, 1787.

4

We the People

of the United States, in Order

re domestic Tranquility, provide for the common defence, promote the general Welfare, a
our Posterity, do ordain and establish this Constitution for the United States of America.

Article. I.

on. 1. All legislative Powers herein granted shall be vested in a Congress of the United S
resentatives.

on. 2. The House of Representatives shall be composed of Members chosen every second Yea
tate shall have the Qualifications requisite for Electors of the most numerous Branch of the State Legis
Person shall be a Representative who shall not have attained to the Age of twenty five Years,
hall not, when elected, be an Inhabitant of that State in which he shall be chosen.
resentatives and direct Taxes shall be apportioned among the several States which may be include
hich shall be determined by adding to the whole Number of free Persons, including those bound t
hree fifths of all other Persons. The actual Enumeration shall be made within three Years after
every subsequent Term of ten Years, in such Manner as they shall by Law direct. The Numbe
nd, but each State shall have at Least one Representative; and until such enumeration shall
ve three; Massachusetts eight; Rhode Island and Providence Plantations one; Connecticut f
ve one; Maryland six; Virginia ten; North Carolina five; South Carolina five; and Georg
Vacancies happen in the Representation from any State, the Executive Authority thereof shall
use of Representatives shall chuse their Speaker and other Officers; and shall have the sole P

he Senate of the United States shall be composed of two Senators from each State, chosen by
ave one Vote.
tely after they shall be assembled in Consequence of the first Election, they shall be divided
the first Class shall be vacated at the Expiration of the second Year, of the second Class at the
tion of the sixth Year, so that one third may be chosen every second Year; and if Vacancies h
ture of any State, the Executive thereof may make temporary Appointments until the next M

shall be a Senator who shall not have attained to the Age of thirty Years, and been nine Year
n Inhabitant of that State for which he shall be chosen.
dent of the United States shall be President of the Senate, but shall have no Vote, unless they
ll chuse their other Officers, and also a President pro tempore, in the Absence of the Vice Pre
States.
l have the sole Power to try all Impeachments. When sitting for that Purpose, they sha
hief Justice shall preside: And no Person shall be convicted without the Concurrence of tw
s of Impeachment shall not extend further than to removal from Office, and d
United States: but the Party convicted shall nevertheless b
Place.

The Supreme Court is one of the three branches of the nation's government. The Constitution's framers wanted a strong federal government. However, they feared putting too much power in one place.

Their solution was to set up a system of checks and balances, also known as the Separation of Powers. This solution came from Virginia's James Madison.

James Madison set up the system of checks and balances known as the "Separation of Powers" for the federal government.

He was a major architect of the Constitution. Madison divided power three ways. He set up a legislative branch (Congress), an executive branch (a President), and a judicial branch (the Supreme Court and the other federal courts).

Section One of Article Three of the Constitution says "The judicial power of the United States, shall be vested in one supreme court, and in such inferior (lower) courts as the Congress may, from time to time, ordain (authorize) and establish."

The first Congress of the United States passed the Judiciary Act on September 24, 1789. This act created a six-member Supreme Court (the superior or high court) and other federal courts, (the inferior or lower courts). The nation's first President, George Washington, appointed John Jay as the first Chief Justice. Washington named five Associate Justices that same year. Since then, the number of justices set by Congress has varied. It was raised from six to ten, lowered to seven, and, since 1870, has been nine.

George Washington appointed John Jay as the first Chief Justice.

Role of the Court

The Constitution in Section Two of Article Three describes the federal courts' power. It does not, however, define that power to any extent. The Supreme Court began to do so early on.

The first two Presidents, Washington and John Adams, and the first Congresses did not really want a judicial branch equal in power.

John Adams appointed John Marshall as the fourth Chief Justice. He believed a strong court system was important.

However, in 1801 Adams appointed Secretary of State John Marshall as the Supreme Court's fourth Chief Justice in 12 years. Marshall believed that a strong court system was important. Under the Constitution, he said, "It is…the province and duty of the judicial department, to say what the law is."

Marshall made this statement in 1803 in the Court's opinion in *Marbury vs. Madison*. This was the first case in which the Court voided a law of Congress. The Court found that particular law inconsistent with the Constitution. To this day, the Supreme Court has followed this precedent. A precedent is a court decision which may be used as a standard to follow in later similar cases.

"The powers of the legislature are defined and limited," Marshall wrote. The Constitution "controls" any law which contradicts it. In establishing the Court's power to limit Congress, Marshall assured that the courts would be very much an equal branch of the government.

The courts' ability to determine if a law is constitutional is called the power of judicial review. This power has since become the public's major image of the Supreme Court. The public sees the Court as the final judge of whether or not a law or government policy conforms with the Constitution.

We ask: Is it "Constitutional?"

One scholar says "there is no 'last word'" on making this judgment. Through the years, times change and different people sit on the Court. New viewpoints are introduced. So, Supreme Court opinions are subject to change. Sometimes, the Court even reverses a previous decision.

Becoming a Justice

Who decides who's going to be a Supreme Court justice?

The Constitution says in Article Two that the President "shall nominate, and by and with the advice and consent of the Senate, shall appoint…judges of the Supreme Court…."

The most recent Court vacancy occurred in June 1991 when Associate Justice Thurgood Marshall resigned. There was the usual talk about the considerations involved in naming a new justice. There are references to tradition and high-minded principles. It is said a President should ignore politics and race or religion. He should just pick the nation's brightest lawyer or judge.

Associate Justice Thurgood Marshall resigned in 1991 creating a vacancy on the Supreme Court that President George Bush had to fill.

After all, the Supreme Court is the nation's final court of appeals. A Court justice is at the top of the power structure in the nation's capital. Shouldn't a Supreme Court nominee be among the Country's outstanding jurists?

Shouldn't a justice be a brilliant legal scholar?

It might seem that's the way it should be, but it seldom happens. A justice is rarely an outstanding jurist or a brilliant scholar. To suggest otherwise, is "historical nonsense," says a researcher.

Throughout the past 200 years, presidents have chosen Supreme Court justices for many reasons. Intelligence or legal skill have not been uppermost among those reasons. Some nominees have been political hacks. Others were chosen primarily because they were friends of the President.

President Reagan kept a campaign promise when, in 1981, he chose Sandra Day O'Connor to be the first female justice.

Sharing a viewpoint similar to a President is almost always a reason a justice is chosen. Most nominees are also members of the President's political party. Only about ten percent of Court nominees have not been a President's political ally.

There have been considerations used in selecting Supreme Court justices.

High among these considerations are religion, where someone lives, and, more recently, a person's race and gender (man or woman).

Judge Clarence Thomas (l) speaks with reporters after President Bush announced that he is nominating Thomas to replace retiring Justice Thurgood Marshall.

From 1932 to 1969 four men held a so-called "Jewish-seat" on the Court. Since 1894 not a year has gone by without a Roman Catholic serving on the Court. President Lyndon B. Johnson selected Marshall in 1967 as the Court's first black justice. President Ronald Reagan kept a campaign promise when in 1981 he chose Sandra Day O'Connor to be the first female justice.

So President George Bush was not out of step with history if he sought a black to replace Marshall. The President denies appointing Thomas because he was black. But most Court observers believe Clarence Thomas' nomination was racially motivated. Was Thomas among the nation's most brilliant legal minds? No one except those most loyal to the President would suggest that. Thomas, however, was a conservative Republican.

The Senate's Role

What about the Senate's role in placing someone on the nation's highest court? The Senate is required by the Constitution to "advise and consent" on court nominations.

What should the Senate consider when reviewing a Court nominee? Should Senators ignore politics or the nominee's judicial philosophy? Should they consider only the nominee's intellectual and moral qualities?

This is the way the selection process has actually worked. If the politics were right, the Senate has confirmed almost all nominees. It has been over 200 years since George Washington took office as the first President of the United States. During that time only 29 men nominated by a president to serve on the Supreme Court did not survive the confirmation process. Only two of them were rejected by the Senate because they were not seen as professionally qualified.

The Senate's consideration of a Supreme Court nominee often focuses on a particular issue. The abortion issue had been the major focal point in recent years. Almost 200 years ago, the issue was the politics associated with a treaty with Britain. As a result, President Washington's 1795 appointee became the first nominee to be rejected.

Lifetime Terms

$\mathscr{S}$ ome Constitutional scholars think the Senate should look more carefully at Court nominees. After all, a seat on the Supreme Court is a very powerful position.

Also, a Court appointee can remain on the court for a long time. All federal justices have lifetime appointments. The Constitution says in Section One of Article Three that "The judges…shall hold their offices during good behavior."

Almost half of all 106 Supreme Court justices have served 15 or more years on the Court. Eleven of them have served 30 to 36 years each. Associate Justice William O. Douglas served the longest. Another 19 were on the Court for 20 to 29 years.

Some of the justices appointed by former President Ronald Reagan and President Bush are likely to be on the Court well into the next century.

The Senate through the years has approached a president's choice for a Court seat with more caution than necessary. At least that's the view of a professor of constitutional law. He says there is no reason for this. Each Senator, the professor says, should make a decision. The Senator should decide "whether that nominee is the right person for the Court."

A sitting Supreme Court justice or federal court judge can be removed from office only by impeachment. To impeach is to charge with misconduct in office. No Supreme Court justice ever has been impeached.

American Courts

Besides the Supreme Court and the other federal courts, all 50 states have their own courts. Within the federal and state court systems there are courts of *original jurisdiction* and *courts of appeals* or appellate courts.

A court of original jurisdiction is where a legal proceeding begins. These courts are called District Courts in the federal system. They have many different names in the state systems, but usually begin with a city court, often called a municipal court. Within the states, they generally include a county or multi-county court, sometimes called a district court.

Article Three of the Constitution says in Section Two that in cases involving representatives of foreign governments or a state the Supreme Court shall have "original jurisdiction." In these instances a legal proceeding begins in a federal court.

Other legal proceedings begin in a state court.

In other cases, the Constitution says, the Supreme Court "shall have the appellate jurisdiction." An appeal is a request to a higher authority. In law, an appeals court is a higher (superior) court where a legal proceeding is transferred from a lower (inferior) court for a rehearing. Most often this transfer results from a request for a review of a lower court decision. Federal appellate courts are called United States Courts of Appeal. There are 12 of them throughout the country. States have various names for appellate courts. In most states, the highest level appeals court is called the Supreme Court.

There are various levels of appellate courts in both the federal system and within the states. The United States Supreme Court is the highest level for both. Most cases heard by the U.S. Supreme Court come from either the federal appellate system or a state supreme court.

U.S. Legal System

The United States legal system includes two major areas – *civil* and *criminal*. Whenever the federal government or a state charges someone with a crime, such as theft or murder, it is a criminal case. Most other lawsuits are civil cases. These are legal proceedings involving the rights of private individuals. A corporation is considered a person under the law.

Civil cases involving residents or businesses within one state usually begin in a court in that state. Those involving residents of different states might originate in a federal court.

Criminal cases are divided broadly into *misdemeanor* and *felony* cases. A misdemeanor charge, such as a traffic violation, carries a lesser penalty than a felony charge. Kidnapping or murder are examples of felony charges. Most criminal charges begin in state courts.

Chance of High Court Review Slim

Supreme Court justices work in the Supreme Court Building on First Street in Washington, D.C. The building occupies an entire block. On the front of the white marble structure are the words: "Equal Justice Under Law." Within the building are the justices' offices, known as chambers. Each justice has a staff which includes young lawyers, called clerks. Much of a justice's time at work is spent reading and writing in chambers.

The Supreme Court's formal work year begins by tradition on the first Monday in October. The Court's annual term ends when the final decision of the term is announced. This is usually the following June. The Court then goes into recess until October.

The Supreme Court itself decides which appeals from lower court decisions it will hear (review). The odds of an appeals being heard are very bad. Each year the Supreme Court receives some 4,000 to 5,000 requests for review. The Court hears only about 150 cases each term.

At least four of the nine justices must vote to hear a case. If the Supreme Court does not review a case, the decision of the lower court stands.

The court meets to study cases for review in an office next to the Chief Justice's chambers. Bookcases full of law books fill the walls of the room. The reviews are secret.

"Equal Justice Under Law" are the words on the Supreme Court building on First Street in Washington, D.C.

Associate Justice Sandra Day O'Connor has discussed decisions about reviewing cases. One consideration, she said, is "the extent to which a Supreme Court ruling on the issue is really needed...."

Once the Court agrees to hear a case, the parties to the case are notified. Attorneys representing both sides file briefs for the justices to study. Briefs are legal documents detailing the parties' positions.

Despite the name, briefs can be thousands of pages. The Court also schedules oral arguments on the case. On the scheduled day, the attorneys involved come to Washington, D.C.

They will try to persuade the justices that the law favors their positions. Arguments are held on Mondays, Tuesdays, and Wednesdays during two weeks each month of a Court term. Two cases are presented in the morning and two more in the afternoon.

The Supreme Court building in Washington, D.C., takes up a city block.

Official Supreme Court sessions, including arguments, are held in a large courtroom. These sessions are open to the public. The courtroom is decorated in marble and mahogany. Twenty-four huge marble columns run along the sides of the room.

The nine justices enter the courtroom after putting on their black robes in another room. Before they enter, the Court clerk says: "All rise!" In the courtroom the justices sit behind a long mahogany table on a raised platform – the court bench. They sit in order of seniority. The Chief Justice sits on the left. The associate justice who has been on the court the longest sits next to him. The newest associate justice sits on the far right.

Each side gets 30 minutes to argue their case. The justices often interrupt the lawyers with questions. Justice O'Connor says the arguments are a great responsibility for a justice. She called it a task to be approached with "awe." Once arguments are heard, it is necessary to determine how each justice might vote on a case. Then the task of writing an opinion can be assigned. An opinion is a formal statement of the Court's reasons for reaching a decision. Viewpoints often change before the entire court agrees on a final decision.

View of a United States Supreme Court chamber in Washington, D.C.

When deciding how to vote, justices consider the history of the case as it has come through the lower court or courts. The justices and their clerks study the briefs and review the oral arguments. They also research past court decisions which relate to the case being reviewed, including precedents. The justices' own personal understandings of Constitutional law impact their decision-making. So do their individual philosophies.

Most of the communication between the justices regarding cases under review is done in writing. On Fridays, the justices meet in private to discuss cases. These meetings are called case conferences.

There is an odd number of justices, so there will be a majority on one side or the other if all state a position. When the Chief Justice is on the majority side, he assigns one of the justices on that side to write the majority *opinion*. The Chief Justice may write the majority opinion himself. If the Chief Justice is in the minority, the most senior justice on the majority side assigns the writing of the majority opinion.

Sometimes a justice on the minority side also writes an opinion. The justice gives his or her reasons for *dissenting* (disagreeing) with the majority opinion. More than one justice may decide to write a dissenting opinion.

One or more justices on the majority side may write a *concurring* opinion. He or she concurs (agrees) with the decision, but perhaps has a different reason for reaching that decision and wants to make that known.

The justice assigned to write an opinion researches the question with the help of the clerks. The opinion writer sends a draft to the other justices for their reaction. The other justices may indicate they will join in the opinion. They also may make suggestions they would like to see included.

Eventually, each justice takes a position. Sometimes the process spreads over more than one term. When positions are firm, final opinions are completed and the Court's decision is announced. Great care is taken to keep the process secret until the decision is made public and the opinion or opinions published.

The opinions are the Supreme Court's most visible work. The justices take this task very seriously. The opinions give the parties involved and the public an understanding of how and why the Court reached a particular decision. Opinions also form the body of law which government agencies and lower courts rely upon.

Is a Court Decision Forever?

Once the Supreme Court makes a decision, will the decision govern forever?

No.

Remember the system of checks and balances? Though the Supreme Court is the court of last appeal, the judicial system is not all powerful. Congress can enact laws which in effect overrule a court decision. However, the new law can be contested in the courts. Then the question again may move through the legal system for another review by the Supreme Court.

A decision may also be overturned by an Amendment to the Constitution. For example, the 14th Amendment (1868) overturned the decision of the 1857 *Dred Scott* case. And the 16th Amendment (1913) overturned *Pollock vs. Farmer's Loan and Trust Company* (1895), which had declared a federal income tax to be unconstitutional.

Sometimes the Supreme Court reverses itself on a particular issue. Reversals occur because the Constitution is necessarily imprecise. The four-page document impacts the present. But the framers of the Constitution lived in a world very different than today.

Applying the meaning of the Constitution to situations in today's world is an imprecise undertaking. As former Supreme Court Justice Oliver Wendell Holmes said of the Constitution: "It is an experiment as all life is an experiment."

$\mathcal{H}$olmes is one of many justices who have made permanent marks on history. However, many others are lost in history.

Holmes has been called a "legendary justice, the living symbol of courage, dignity and eloquence." He served on the Supreme Court for 29 years, retiring in 1932 at age 90.

When Holmes retired, there was a groundswell for the appointment of Benjamin Cardozo to fill the vacancy. Cardozo, in his early 60s, was the chief appellate judge in New York State. Cardozo was Jewish and there was one Jewish justice on the Court. Cardozo was a New Yorker and there were two New Yorkers on the Court. Cardozo also was a Democrat. Republican President Herbert Hoover appointed him anyway. Justice Cardozo served only six years, but most Court experts say he was "the greatest legal mind ever on the Supreme Court."

Oliver Wendall Holmes served on the Supreme Court for 29 years and was considered a "legendary justice."

39

Earlier, between 1801 and 1835, Chief Justice John Marshall made a strong mark on the Court.

Chief Justice Earl Warren served from 1953-1959. He led the Court to a liberal stance. He authored *Brown vs. Board of Education of Topeka, Kansas*, a landmark 1954 decision banning segregation in school. Warren was a Republican who had been governor of California. He was a political Court appointment of President Dwight D. Eisenhower.

Experts say that Benjamin Cardoza was "the greatest legal mind ever on the Supreme Court."

Warren had no judicial experience when appointed.

William J. Brennan Jr. served as an Associate Justice from 1956-1990. During his long tenure, Brennan watched the Court move to the left under Chief Justice Warren. Then he saw it move to the right under Chief Justices Warren E. Burger and William H. Rehnquist.

Brennan became the Supreme Court's leading liberal jurist. He was 84 when he retired. A biographer says his "vote and intellectual contributions helped turn the tide" in many landmark criminal law rulings.

Chief Justice Earl Warren was a former governor of California. He served from 1953-1959.

Brennan's "stamina, intellect and political (savvy) have combined to distinguish him as undisputedly one of the most influential jurists in the history of the Court."

Thurgood Marshall was the Court's first black justice. For 24 years (1967-1991), he also was "a conscience on the bench." A reporter said Marshall was "never wavering in his devotion to ending discrimination."

Marshall was an activist civil rights lawyer before President Lyndon B. Johnson appointed him to the Court. In the Warren Court, Marshall was in the middle, part of a liberal majority. By the time he retired at age 82, Marshall was at the far left of the conservative Rehnquist Court.

Other famous Supreme Court associate justices include John Harlan, who served from 1877 to 1911. Louis D. Brandeis served from 1916 to 1939. Harlan F. Stone was a justice from 1925 to 1941.

Hugo L. Black, a justice from 1937 to 1971, was one of only four Baptists ever to serve on the Court. Felix Frankfurter, born in Austria, was on the Court from 1939 to 1962. William O. Douglas served on the Court for 36 years from 1939 to 1975.

Justice William Brennan became the Supreme Court's leading liberal jurist. He was 84 when he retired.

The Court Today

The Supreme Court was for white males only for 178 years until Thurgood Marshall became the 97th justice in 1967. As 1992 began, the Court included its first woman member (O'Connor), the first Italian American (Associate Justice Antonin Scalia), and the second black (Thomas).

Although there has been a Jewish justice for most of this century, there is none at present. Four justices attend an Episcopal Church. Two are Catholic. There is a Lutheran, a Methodist, and Associate Justice John Paul Stevens is listed as a Protestant.

Through the years, the Court has been dominated by men from the East Coast. Today two justices spent much of their lives in Arizona. One is from California, one from Colorado, and one grew up in Georgia. Two are from the Midwest – Illinois and Minnesota. Only Associate Justices Scalia and David Souter are from the East Coast.

Most of the current justices are wealthy. Some are millionaires.

Today's court, says *Time* magazine, pushes a conservative stance. Under Chief Justice Earl Warren, the Court was very liberal. This change has taken place over many years. Many believe the Court is ready now to change some of its past major rulings.

Chief Justice Rehnquist spearheaded the conservative switchover. He is generally joined by Justices Kennedy, O'Connor, and Scalia. David Souter, the second newest justice, has provided an important fifth vote on some notable cases. Justice Thomas is expected to reveal a conservative viewpoint. The Court is not likely to veer left for a long time. Of the above six justices, one is in his 40s, three are in their 50s, and two are in their 60s. All six were appointed by Republican Presidents.

So was Justice Stevens. He and Justice White form the shrunken middle of the Court. Justice White is the only Court member named by a Democrat President (John F. Kennedy).

Justice White can be expected to join the conservative majority on cases involving criminal law and police powers. Justice Stevens supports the conservatives on some free-speech matters. Justice Stevens and White are in their 70s. That leaves 83-year-old Justice Harry Blackmun as the only liberal remaining on the Court.

There is only one question about the present Court: how far will they go in making changes? Change is expected on abortion. Other issues to be watched are church-state relations, individual liberties, and the rights of criminal defendants.

Glossary

Checks and Balances: The legal means used by each branch of the government to limit the powers of the other branches, so that no person or group will have too much power.

Congress: The lawmaking body of the United States of America.

Conservative: Inclined to keep things as they are or were in the past.

Constitution: The fundamental law of a state which guides and limits the use of power by the government.

Impeach: To accuse a public official of wrong conduct while in office. The official is removed from office if found guilty.

Justice: The determination of rights according to the rules of law.

Law: A rule of conduct or action prescribed or formally recognized as binding or enforced by a ruling authority.

Legislature: The branch of government that is charged with such powers as making laws.

Liberal: A person favorable to progress or reform.

Senate: A governing or lawmaking assembly. The Congress of the United States is the Senate and the House of Representatives.

United States Court of Appeals: A court hearing appeals from the decisions of lower courts.

United States Supreme Court: The highest court in the United States, which meets in Washington, D.C. It consists of eight associate justices and one chief justice.

Index

Adams, John-10,11

Bush, George-14,18,19,22

Cardoza, Benjamin-39-41

Civil cases- 26

Congress- 7,8,10,12

Constitution-
4,5,7,10,12,14,20,21,24,25,36,37

Courts of Appeal- 24,25

Criminal cases-26

Holmes, Oliver Wendall-36-39

Jay, John- 8,9

Madison, James-6,7

Marshall, Thurgood-14,15,18,19,43,46

Maybury vs. Madison-10

O'Connor, Sandra Day-17,18,30,31,46,47

Scalia, Antonin- 46-47

Senate- 14,20,22

Stevens, John-46-48

Systems of checks and balances-7,36

Thomas, Clarence- 18,19,46,47

Warren, Earl-41-43,47

Washington, George-8-10,20,21